◆ MARC BROWN ◆

WHAT DO YOU CALL A DUMB BUNNY?

AND OTHER RABBIT RIDDLES, GAMES, JOKES, AND CARTOONS

JOY STREET BOOKS
LITTLE, BROWN AND COMPANY
◆ BOSTON ◆ TORONTO ◆

TWO RABBITS RIDING A BRONTOSAURUS.

THIS BOOK IS FOR ALL THE KIDS WHO SHARED THEIR FAVORITE JOKES WITH ME.

Library of Congress Cataloging in Publication Data

Brown, Marc Tolon.
  What do you call a dumb bunny?

  Summary: A collection of rabbit humor and puzzles, including some illustrated facts about rabbits.
  1. Rabbits – Anecdotes, facetiae, satire, etc.
  2. Wit and humor, Juvenile. [1. Rabbits – Wit and humor.
  2. Rabbits – Miscellanea] I. Title.
PN6231.R23B7 1983   818'.5402   82-21650
ISBN 0-316-11117-1
ISBN 0-316-11119-8 (pbk.)
HC: 10 9 8 7 6 5 4
PB: 10 9 8 7 6 5

JOY STREET BOOKS ARE PUBLISHED BY LITTLE, BROWN AND COMPANY (INC.)

BP

Published simultaneously in Canada by Little, Brown & Company (Canada) Limited

PRINTED IN THE UNITED STATES OF AMERICA

WHAT HAS TWO FUZZY PINK EARS AND WRITES?

I'VE ALREADY HEARD THAT ONE, A BALLPOINT BUNNY.

PLUS A RACE BETWEEN A HARE AND A TORTOISE.

AND TWO FLIP BOOKS, ONE IS A HAIR RAISING EXPERIENCE!

CONTENTS

HOW CAN YOU TELL WHICH RABBITS ARE THE OLDEST IN A GROUP?

JUST LOOK FOR THE GRAY HARES.

WHAT DO YOU CALL A LINE OF RABBITS WALKING BACKWARD?

A RECEDING HARELINE.

HOW DO YOU KNOW CARROTS ARE GOOD FOR YOUR EYES?

HAVE YOU EVER SEEN A RABBIT WITH GLASSES?

FAMOUS RABBITS

RABBITSON CRUSOE

LEONARDO DA VABBIT

RABBITSTEIN'S MONSTER

THOMAS ALVA RABBITSON

RUDOLPH THE RED NOSED RABBIT

RABBIT HOOD

PROFESSOR HARE BRAIN'S RABBIT QUIZ

TRUE OR FALSE

1. SOME RABBITS CAN JUMP 15 FEET.

2. RABBITS' TEETH GROW 4 INCHES EACH YEAR - THAT'S WHY THEY NIBBLE SO MUCH.

3. WHAT IS A RABBIT'S FAVORITE MOVIE MUSICAL?

4. MOST RABBITS LIVE 5 OR 6 YEARS BUT SOME LIVE 13 YEARS.

5. RABBITS HAVE BEEN KNOWN TO HIDE IN TREES.

6. RABBITS LIVE IN SWAMPS, MARSHES, DESERTS, AND FORESTS.

7. RABBITS WITH WHITE FUR AND PINK EYES ARE CALLED ALBINOS.

8. FOR 2000 YEARS PEOPLE HAVE TAMED RABBITS FOR PETS.

9. MOST RABBITS SHED THEIR COAT THREE OR FOUR TIMES A YEAR.

10. A RABBIT'S FAVORITE FEEDING TIME IN THE WILD IS DAWN OR DUSK.

(ANSWERS: 1,2,4,5,6,7,8,9,10 ALL TRUE. 3, HARE)

THE EASTER BUNNY

THE FIRST EASTER BUNNY MAY HAVE LOOKED SOMETHING LIKE THIS. THE IDEA OF THE EASTER BUNNY IS VERY OLD. IT BEGAN IN ANCIENT EGYPT WHERE THE HARE WAS THE SYMBOL OF THE MOON. THE DATE OF EASTER DEPENDS ON THE MOON.

2 WAYS TO HOLD A RABBIT

NEVER PICK UP A RABBIT BY THE EARS.

HARES AND RABBITS ARE DIFFERENT

HARE
- LARGE SIZE
- LONG EARS
- FAST RUNNER
- COLOR CHANGES WITH THE SEASON
- ARE BORN WITH FUR
- CAN SEE AT BIRTH
- CAN RUN SHORTLY AFTER BIRTH

RABBIT
- SMALL SIZE
- SHORT EARS
- NOT A DISTANCE RUNNER
- COLOR STAYS THE SAME
- NOT BORN WITH FUR
- BORN BLIND
- BORN TOO WEAK TO RUN

MUNCHY MAZE

BOTH HARES AND RABBITS ARE VEGETARIANS. GO THROUGH THE MAZE AND DISCOVER WHAT THEY LIKE TO EAT.

LEAVES, CLOVER, ALFALFA, LETTUCE, CARROTS, OATS, DANDELIONS, CABBAGE, HAY, GARDEN PLANTS, KALE, BRAN, GRASS, BOILED POTATOES

YUM YUM

HOW MANY RABBITS CAN YOU FIT IN AN EMPTY PHONE BOOTH?

TELEPHONE

ONE. AFTER THAT IT ISN'T EMPTY.

WHAT DO RABBITS GET WHEN IT RAINS?

WET

WHY CAN A RABBIT HOP HIGHER THAN THE EMPIRE STATE BUILDING?

THE EMPIRE STATE BUILDING CAN'T HOP.

HOW CAN YOU TELL A RABBIT FROM A GORILLA?

A RABBIT DOESN'T LOOK LIKE A GORILLA.

WHAT KINDS OF RABBITS EAT WITH THEIR EARS?

ALL RABBITS EAT WITH THEIR EARS, THEY CAN'T TAKE THEM OFF

WHAT KIND OF BOOK DOES A RABBIT LIKE AT BEDTIME?

ONE WITH A HOPPY ENDING

THREE LITTLE BUNNIES

DRAW YOUR OWN RABBIT

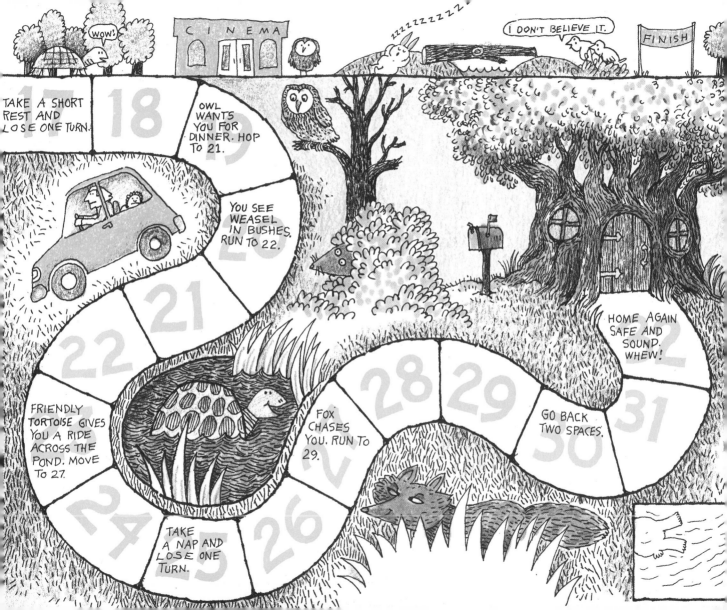

WHAT A DUMB BUNNY!
DINER

CLOSE ENCOUNTERS
OF THE FUZZY KIND

U.F.B.
← UNIDENTIFIED FLYING BUNNY

BUNNY'S
TRUCK STOP
EAT HERE
GET GAS

CRUNCHY CARROT INC.

GAS PETROL   GAS PETROL

CAN WE GET SOME GAS?

LOOK!

I DIDN'T SEE IT.

OH SURE, JUST EAT THE CHILI.

WAITRESS, WHAT'S THIS HARE DOING IN MY SOUP?

LOOKS LIKE THE BACKSTROKE.

LET ME OUT, THIS PLACE IS GROSS.

WHAT A DUMP.

BURP.

PLAY THE PIANO

THE SECRET LIFE OF RABBITS
THINGS YOU NEVER SEE RABBITS DO

FLY A KITE

PLAY DRESS·UP

RIDE A SKATEBOARD

RIDE A TRICYCLE

HOW TO MAKE A RABBIT SHADOW

GET SOME OF YOUR FRIENDS TOGETHER AND MAKE SOME RABBIT SHADOWS OR HAVE A RABBIT SHADOW PLAY. SEE HOW MANY OTHER SHADOW ANIMALS YOU CAN MAKE WITH YOUR HANDS.

RIDICULOUS RABBIT DISGUISES

HUMAN NOSE

WILD GLASSES

MOUSTACHE

FANGS

HUMAN EARS

BEARD

MONSTER RABBIT

BAD BUNNY

GOOD GUY

REGULAR RABBIT

TAB   TAB

ASTRO BUNNY

A

WITCH RABBIT

MAKE YOUR OWN FINGER PUPPETS
TRACE AND COLOR, THEN CUT OUT AND TAPE TABS TOGETHER.
MAKE UP SOME OF YOUR OWN CHARACTERS AND STORIES. HAVE FUN!